Comptroller of the Currency
Administrator of National Banks

I0448357

Insider Activities

Comptroller's Handbook

March 2006

M

Management

Corporate Governance
Insider Activities

Table of Contents

Introduction

This "Insider Activities" booklet is one of several booklets in the *Comptroller's Handbook* that will be published under the theme of corporate governance. This booklet provides guidance on how banks may legally and prudently engage in transactions with insiders and implement risk management processes that provide for the appropriate control and monitoring of insider activities. This booklet also provides guidance on how examiners will review and assess insider activities during the supervisory process.

A bank should engage in safe and sound business and personal transactions with its insiders, consistent with law and regulation. Transactions between a bank and its insiders can address legitimate banking needs and serve the interests of both parties. The challenge is to separate legitimate insider financial relationships from those that are, or could become, abusive, imprudent, or preferential. Studies of bank failures have found that insider abuse, including excessive or poor quality loans made, and unjustified fees paid, to directors and officers, is often a contributing factor to the failure. Because of the significant risks that insider activities can pose, activities are subject to strict laws and ethical guidelines.

While most risks can be measured and quantified, insider abuse can damage a bank's reputation beyond the dollar amount of any credit loss. Improper insider activities can undermine public confidence in the institution. Market perception of the integrity of a bank's insiders is fundamental to the bank's financial health and ongoing viability. To maintain this public confidence, a bank must have a reputation for honesty and integrity in all of its activities, especially in its transactions with insiders.

The bank's corporate governance processes should comprehensively address insider activities. The board of directors must assume leadership by adopting and administering strong written insider policies that closely govern the relationship between the bank and all insiders. The board must also ensure that a process is implemented to monitor and validate compliance with these policies. As used in this booklet, the definition of "insider" is broader than the regulatory definition of a bank insider. Unless otherwise noted, the word "insider" in this booklet is intended to mean an institution-affiliated party, such as an officer, director, employee, controlling shareholder, and all "related interests" of these persons. Regulation O (12 CFR 215), which imposes limits on a bank's loans to insiders, defines the word "insider" more narrowly.

When the word "management" is used in this booklet, it refers to persons who are appointed by the board of directors and charged with the daily responsibilities of operating the bank. When the term "the board and management" is used in this booklet, it refers collectively to the members of the board of directors and management.

Risks Associated with Insider Activities

Examiners assess risk in relation to its impact on capital and earnings. From a supervisory perspective, risk is the potential that events, expected or unanticipated, may have an adverse impact on the bank's earnings or capital. The OCC has identified nine risks for supervisory purposes: credit, interest rate, liquidity, price, foreign currency translation, compliance, transaction, strategic, and reputation. Each risk is defined in the "Bank Supervision Process" booklet of the *Comptroller's Handbook*.

The risks most often associated with insider activities are reputation, credit, liquidity, and compliance risk.

Reputation Risk

The board and management must act at all times in a manner that maintains the bank's reputation for honesty and integrity. Real or perceived insider abuse can severely affect a bank's ability to continue to do business in a profitable manner. When a bank is closely associated with an insider or a company owned by an insider (even if they do not transact business together), the bank may suffer loss of business or other harm if the insider or the insider's business experiences financial difficulties or receives adverse publicity. Any damage to a bank's reputation, or any implication of insider abuse or fraud, may dramatically affect the opinion of the bank's shareholders, customers, suppliers, and financial partners, and may result in a loss of confidence in the bank. In turn, the bank's customer base could erode, materially affecting the bank's earnings and capital.

Credit Risk

Bank insiders are allowed, with certain restrictions, to borrow from the bank.

However, the bank must ensure that lending to insiders is at "arm's length," i.e., on terms and conditions no less stringent than those offered to the general public. The one exception to this general "arm's length" requirement is set forth in Regulation O, which provides that insiders (as defined for Regulation O purposes) may take advantage of benefit and compensation programs widely available to bank employees, as long as any loans made pursuant to such a program are not on terms any less stringent than loans to employees who are not insiders. Loans to insiders could create added credit risk to the bank when inadequate or lax enforcement of insider policies allows for special treatment of insiders who might not otherwise qualify for credit. In addition, pressure from insiders to relax credit standards for their related interests or for their friends' interests can also cause problems. Lending to non-creditworthy insiders, offering inappropriate terms to insiders, or otherwise allowing an environment conducive to insider abuse increases the possibility of loss and violations of law and regulation to the bank.

Liquidity Risk

Any speculation questioning the honesty or integrity of the bank or its insiders, however unfounded, can affect the bank's ability to continue to attract funds from the public, institutional suppliers, and correspondent banks. Even the appearance of insider impropriety could fuel a "run" on the bank and could force the bank to dispose of assets at unacceptable losses in order to maintain liquidity.

Compliance Risk

A bank's board and management are responsible for ensuring that the bank complies with laws, regulations, prescribed practices, and ethical standards. Noncompliance with these requirements or safety and soundness standards can expose the bank and its insiders to serious consequences, including enforcement action. An insider who, knowingly or unknowingly, violates any banking law or regulation, engages in an unsafe or unsound banking practice, or breaches a fiduciary duty may be subject to civil money penalties and removal from banking, and may be held personally liable for any loss incurred by the bank due to such activity.

Duties of the Board and Management

The board and management have a number of duties relating to insider activities. The board's primary responsibilities are to provide strategic leadership and oversight of management. The board should ensure management effectively performs the following duties:

- Establishing appropriate insider policies, including a code of ethics.
- Fulfilling fiduciary obligations relating to common law, including the duty of care and the duty of loyalty.
- Complying with insider-related laws and regulations.
- Establishing and applying sound, independent processes to monitor and ensure compliance with insider policies, laws, and regulations, e.g., providing for effective internal controls and adequate audit coverage.
- Ensuring that hiring practices are effective.
- Setting appropriate compensation and fees paid to insiders.
- Following prudent dividend policies.
- Implementing sound management information systems.
- Submitting accurate financial reports and other disclosures.

Fulfilling these duties should enable the bank to conduct its insider activities in a safe and sound manner.

Policies

Corporate scandals and failures exemplify the need for comprehensive insider policies, including a code of ethics and sound business practices. A corporate culture of ethical and honest behavior, as well as effective board oversight and management supervision, is a bank's primary defense against insider abuse and fraud. Comprehensive insider policies will help establish this culture by setting a standard of behavior for all insiders. A bank's board and management must take the lead in demonstrating ethical behavior of the highest order and protecting the bank from conflicts of interest. Such a "tone at the top" emphasizes personal integrity and accountability while acknowledging the importance of an effective control environment. Board members and other insiders should conduct business with the bank according to an established governance structure that recognizes and observes all of the requirements set forth in the bank's insider policies. Moreover, adherence to these policies should facilitate compliance with all legal and internal requirements for insider relationships.

The policies should focus on the activities of controlling shareholders, directors, officers, and employees at all levels of the bank. They should apply to the bank's interaction with all affiliated parties. Once policies are developed and approved by the board, the board and management should ensure that the policies are communicated throughout the bank. The bank should also have a process to monitor compliance with those policies.

The insider policies and principles should:

- Include a code of ethics that requires the disclosure of actual or potential conflicts of interest.[1]
- Identify all insider "related interests," as that term is defined in Regulation O.
- Require identification of material interests insiders have in the business of any borrower, applicant, other bank customer, vendor, or supplier.
- Include guidelines for insider lending and other transactions, including fees or commissions received from the bank.
- Require that transactions with insiders be at arm's length.
- Require the prompt reporting of insider securities transactions[2].
- Prohibit the use of insider information in securities transactions.
- Specify the circumstances and conditions under which the bank will make its facilities, real or personal property (e.g., airplanes, cars), or personnel available for insiders' use.
- Specify restrictions on the acceptance of gifts, bequests, or other items of value (e.g., an exchange of "favors," payment for services, etc.) from customers or other persons doing or seeking to do business with the bank.
- Require bank employees to report improper or unethical behavior to appropriate parties (bank management, board, auditors, etc.) and to report suspicious activity in accordance with the bank's suspicious activity report (SAR) policy.

---

[1] Companies whose securities are listed with the Securities Exchange Commission are required to disclose whether they have adopted a code of ethics that applies to the company's principal executive officer, principal financial officer, principal accounting officer or controller, or person performing similar functions. If the company has not adopted a code of ethics, it must disclose why it has not done so.

[2] Companies whose securities are listed with the SEC are required to make real-time electronic disclosures relating to insider changes in ownership.

- Specify the consequences of breaches of fiduciary duty and unethical conduct.
- Include guidelines for reporting all insider and insider related transactions to the board of directors or a committee thereof.
- Include recordkeeping requirements established by federal or state law.

The amount of detail in the written insider policies should correspond to the volume and nature of the insider activities the board is willing to accept, and to any applicable legal requirements. The written policies should be sufficiently detailed to enable all affected individuals to fully understand the nature and extent of their responsibilities under the policies. For example, if a bank's policy prohibits all loans to, and any transactions with, insiders, the written policy needs to clearly state that prohibition. If the policy permits loans to, or other transactions with, insiders, the written policy should identify the types of loans and transactions authorized, dollar or other limits, and the approval processes to be followed.

Management should provide all insiders with copies of the bank's written policies and any subsequent changes to these policies. Each insider should sign an acknowledgment that they have received the written policies and code of ethics, any subsequent change to the policies, and an agreement to comply with the policies. It is management's responsibility to maintain a file of these signed acknowledgements at the bank.

To foster compliance with laws, regulations, and insider policies, the bank should develop training and awareness programs covering insider issues. The bank should consider establishing communication channels outside the normal chain of command through which insiders can seek advice on questions about the insider policies, conflicts of interest, or similar concerns. If such support is readily available, insiders are more likely to seek guidance. Management should monitor questions and responses to ensure that answers and interpretations are consistent and conform to bank policy and applicable legal requirements. Educational and training opportunities may be available from local, state, and national trade associations.

Duty of Care and Duty of Loyalty

In addition to the specific laws and regulations discussed in this booklet, insider activities are governed by fiduciary principles of common law—the body of law made up of cases decided by the courts.

The common law establishes generally accepted fiduciary legal principles and it imposes two basic duties on management and the board – the "duty of care" and the "duty of loyalty." Under the duty of care, management and the board must diligently and honestly administer the bank's affairs in a manner measured against what a reasonable and prudent person would do in similar circumstances. Under the duty of loyalty, management and the board must place the corporate interests of the bank above their personal interests. Many banks, as a matter of policy, have expanded the application of the common law duties to all employees.

Under the duty of care, the courts usually hold a director responsible for knowing what a reasonable and prudent director would have known, and the courts evaluate the director's conduct based on that knowledge. When a court examines whether a director has fulfilled the duty of care, the court will measure the director's conduct against the applicable standard established by law. Failure to exercise the duty of care may subject a director to personal liability.

The duty of loyalty requires directors and management to act in the best interests of the bank and to ensure that insiders do not abuse their positions by benefiting personally at the bank's expense. In general, a conflict of interest exists when the personal or business interests of insiders are inconsistent with the continued safe and sound operation of the bank or with a business opportunity of the institution. Insiders should avoid placing themselves in a position that creates a conflict of interest or the appearance of a conflict of interest. For example, a director or officer has a conflicting interest in a transaction if he or she appears on both sides of the transaction or derives any personal benefit from it in the sense of self-dealing. A conflict of interest can also exist if a director or officer has such a substantial interest outside of the bank that it could reasonably affect his or her judgment with respect to the bank's business. Such a conflict of interest may arise out of one's personal business interests and/or in connection with transactions that benefit friends, relatives or business associates.

A bank's relationship with its insiders must at all times be prudent, at "arm's length" and in compliance with all applicable laws and regulations. Management and members of the board must fully disclose any personal interest that they may have in matters affecting the bank and must ensure that these business and personal relationships with the bank are always at arm's length. Disinterested directors should approve transactions involving the interests of other affiliated parties, and directors should abstain from voting and deliberating on any matter involving their own interests. Banks should note that, with respect to loans that are subject to Regulation O's "prior board approval" requirement (12 CFR 215.4(b)), a majority of the *entire* board must approve the loan.

The "usurpation of corporate opportunity" doctrine, a part of the duty of loyalty, prevents insiders from improperly taking business opportunities away from the bank.

Independence and unbiased decision making are important aspects of the duty of loyalty. As a result, the SEC requires a majority of directors of public companies to be independent of management and all members of the audit committee of public companies to be independent of management.[3]

These duties and obligations are described in more detail in *The Director's Book*, published by the OCC. For additional information on audit committee requirements, refer to the "Internal and External Audits" booklet of the *Comptroller's Handbook*.

A director who violates any banking law or regulation, engages in an unsafe or unsound banking practice, or breaches a fiduciary duty (or permits another person to do so) may be held personally liable and may be subject to civil money penalties, administrative actions, or other sanctions. The director may be held responsible either alone or jointly with other board members.

Holding Companies and Other Affiliates

The board of directors and management of a bank often include many of the same people on the board and management team of the bank's parent company. It is not uncommon for the board and management of a bank subsidiary of a one-bank holding company to be the same as that of the holding company, particularly in community bank situations. Similarly, the directors and officers of a multi-bank holding company with centralized operations (or the directors and officers of the lead bank) often head each of the holding company's bank subsidiaries. The holding company or lead bank usually controls such activities as investment portfolio management, budgeting, tax planning, personnel management, correspondent banking, loan participations, and asset-liability management. While such structures

---

[3] The FDIC established a similar requirement for the audit committees of banks with total assets of $1 billion.

can benefit the bank, persons who serve in dual capacities can develop conflicting loyalties.

Corporate governance policies should recognize this potential for divided loyalties, and should provide guidance for preventing and resolving such conflicts of interest. The overriding principle must be that the bank subsidiary is not disadvantaged by a transaction with its holding company, any other affiliate, or any insider. Certain transactions with affiliates are subject to legal limitations. See the "Related Organizations" booklet of the *Comptroller's Handbook* for further discussion of this issue.

Compliance with Insider Laws and Regulations

In addition to the duties imposed by common law, various statutes and regulations govern insider activities. Unlike the broad standards in common law, these laws and regulations are specific about how insiders are to conduct themselves. Since the statutory and regulatory restrictions on insider transactions do not apply uniformly to all insiders, the board and management must become familiar with each restriction and must pay careful attention to the scope and import of each.

12 CFR 215 – Regulation O

Regulation O, the Federal Reserve Board's regulation that implements many of the laws pertaining to bank insider transactions, including 12 USC 375a and 375b, is the most comprehensive banking regulation relating to extensions of credit to insiders. It limits the amount and type of credit that may be extended, and includes reporting and record keeping requirements. The term "insider" has a special definition for purposes of Regulation O. For purposes of most of subpart A of Regulation O, the term "insider" includes a "principal shareholder," an "executive officer," a "director," and the "related interests" of any of these persons. A "related interest" of a person includes (1) a company that is controlled by that person, or (2) a political or campaign committee that is controlled by that person or the funds or services of which will benefit that person. All of these terms are further defined by 12 CFR 215.2. These definitions, however, do not apply to *all* provisions of Regulation O, so banks must be careful in determining the persons or entities subject to a particular Regulation O provision. The term "extension of credit" is also specifically and broadly defined by Regulation O and includes loan renewals. See 12 CFR 215.3 and appendix B of this booklet. Regulation O's six main provisions include:

- A prohibition on loans to insiders unless a loan (1) is non-preferential **and** (2) does not present a higher-than-normal risk of repayment or other unfavorable features.[4]
- A requirement that prior board approval is obtained for loans to insiders greater than a certain amount.
- A limit on lending to individual insiders and to insiders in aggregate.
- Restrictions on loans to executive officers in other ways.
- A requirement that insiders report and disclose certain financial information.
- A requirement that certain insiders report and disclose indebtedness to correspondent banks.

Most violations of 12 USC 375a, 375b, or 1972(2) will also be violations of Regulation O. When determining compliance with the quantitative limits of Regulation O, examiners and bankers must make sure they use the definition of unimpaired capital and unimpaired surplus in Regulation O[5].

12 USC 375

This statute prohibits the bank from engaging in preferential sales or purchases of securities or other property with directors or any firm of which a director is a member. Transactions with directors involving securities or other property are allowed only if (a) the sale or purchase is made in the regular course of business and the terms are comparable to those afforded the general public for the same securities or other property, or (b) the transaction is approved by a majority of the disinterested members of the board. However, compliance with section 375 does not absolve directors from the need to comply with their fiduciary duties.

12 USC 375a

---

[4] OCC Interpretive Letter 1024. A loan to an insider that has become troubled may not be renewed unless the lending bank obtains additional protection to safeguard it and offset the unfavorable features the loan would otherwise present. Depending on the facts, a bank could require additional collateral, a guarantee, or other credit enhancement.

[5] Regulation O defines unimpaired capital and unimpaired surplus as the sum of Tier 1 and Tier 2 capital included in the bank's risk-based capital, based on the bank's most recent call report, and the balance of the bank's allowance for loan and lease losses not included in Tier 2 capital for risk-based capital purposes, based on the bank's most recent call report. 12 CFR 215.2(i)

Section 375a limits extensions of credit to executive officers (but not to their related interests). Mortgage loans are permitted regardless of amount if the loan is secured by a first lien on a dwelling the executive officer owns and uses as a residence. ***Executive officers may have only one such loan outstanding at a time.*** Extensions of credit to finance children's education are also permitted without limit. Other loans, although permitted, are subject to a lending limit set by 12 CFR 215.5(c)(4), Regulation O. Additional restrictions on loans to executive officers are imposed by 12 USC 375b as discussed below. Thus, mortgage and educational loans are not limited by section 375a, but aggregate loans to an individual executive officer and to insiders and their related interests collectively are limited by section 375b and section 215.4 of Regulation O.

12 USC 375b

Section 375b applies limits and prohibitions to extensions of credit made by a bank to all insiders – executive officers, directors, and principal shareholders, and the related interests of these persons. The statute prohibits preferential lending, high-risk loans, and certain types of overdrafts. It also requires prior board approval for large loans, and limits aggregate loans to individual insiders and to all insiders as a group.

Individual Insiders

Aggregate loans and extensions of credit to each executive officer, director, or principal shareholder and his or her related interests are limited to the single borrower limit in 12 USC 84. A bank's loans to related interests of an insider are attributed to that insider and are combined with any other loans to that insider outstanding from the bank regardless of whether or not such loans are combinable under the legal lending limit combination rule of 12 CFR 32.5.

All Insiders

Total extensions of credit to all insiders and their related interests are limited to the amount of the bank's unimpaired capital and unimpaired surplus. Banks with deposits of less than $100 million are subject to a higher limit if they meet certain qualifications. That limit is equal to a total of two times the bank's unimpaired capital and unimpaired surplus, subject to restrictions specified in 12 CFR 215.4(d).

Exceptions to the limits on aggregate loans to individual insiders are available for any loan type that is eligible for a higher limit under 12 USC 84. Exceptions to the limit on aggregate loans to insiders as a group are made for extensions of credit:

- Secured or fully guaranteed by obligations of the United States.
- To, or secured by, qualified commitments or guarantees of, a department or agency of the United States.
- Secured by a segregated deposit account with the lending bank.
- Arising from the discount of installment consumer paper acquired from an insider with recourse under certain conditions.

12 USC 376

Section 376 prohibits the payment of preferential interest on deposits to any director, officer, attorney, or employee of the bank.

12 USC 1972(2)

Section 1972(2) prohibits a bank and its correspondent bank from making preferential loans and loans that involve more than the normal risk of repayment or present other unfavorable terms to an insider of the other bank. It also prohibits a bank from opening a correspondent account at another bank where either bank has outstanding a preferential loan, or a loan that involves more than the normal risk of repayment or presents other unfavorable features, to an insider of the other.

Internal Controls and Audit

Internal or external audits should complement the bank's internal controls and information systems. Such functions should be sufficient to detect actual conflicts of interest and the risk of insider abuse. The board should ensure that management has implemented a process to monitor compliance with insider laws, regulations, and bank policy.

A system of strong internal controls is critical to ensuring compliance with bank policies and with laws and regulations concerning insider transactions. A sound internal control system minimizes the possibility of significant errors and irregularities, and ensures timely detection of those that do occur. The board, through its oversight role, should ensure that the bank's system of internal controls and audit alerts the bank to the following practices or conditions:

- Transactions resulting in a conflict of interest or the appearance of such a conflict.
- The payment of excessive compensation or unjustified fees.
- Failure to comply with laws, regulations, or bank-imposed restrictions.

If any of these practices or conditions is discovered, the board should determine the cause, instruct management to take appropriate corrective action, and oversee necessary revisions to policies or internal controls.

For additional guidance and requirements regarding management and Board responsibilities for establishing and maintaining an effective internal control structure and complying with safety and soundness laws concerning transactions with insiders, refer to the "Internal and External Audits" booklet of the Comptroller's Handbook; 12 CFR 363, Annual Independent Audits and Reporting Requirements; and section 404 of the Sarbanes-Oxley Act. [6]

Compensation and Benefits Paid to Insiders

Compensation and fees paid to insiders must serve the legitimate needs of the bank, must be justified by the services rendered, and must be reasonable in amount. In assessing this area, all forms of remuneration, including salary, fees, benefits, stock options and the receipt of other goods and services, should be considered.

As set forth in interagency guidelines, banks should maintain safeguards to prevent the payment of compensation, fees, and benefits that are excessive or that could lead to material financial loss to the bank. (See 12 CFR Part 30, Appendix A: Interagency Guidelines Prescribing Standards for Safety and Soundness.) An insider's compensation is considered excessive, and is therefore prohibited as an unsafe and unsound practice, if it is unreasonable or disproportionate to the services actually performed. The following factors should be considered in determining whether compensation is excessive:

---

[6] Under Section 301 of Sarbanes-Oxley, the audit committees of public companies are required to establish procedures for (a) the receipt, retention, and treatment of complaints received by the issuer regarding accounting, internal accounting controls, or auditing matters; and for (b) the issuer's employees to submit information about questionable accounting or auditing matters in a confidential, anonymous manner.

- The combined value of all cash and non-cash benefits provided to the individual in relation to the services rendered.
- The compensation history of the individual and other individuals with comparable expertise and responsibilities at the institution.
- The financial condition of the institution, including reasonable projections.
- Compensation practices at comparable institutions, based upon such factors as asset size, geographic location, and the complexity of the bank's asset mix, products, and services.
- For post-employment benefits, the projected total cost and benefit to the institution.
- Any other relevant factors.

As noted above, compensation packages may include non-cash benefits. One such permissible non-cash benefit is a bank's purchase of directors and officers liability insurance. This insurance protects against the expense of defending lawsuits (and paying related damages) alleging director or officer misconduct. Some of this insurance reimburses the bank for payments made to directors and officers under indemnification agreements, and the rest reimburses the directors and officers for expenses that the bank is unable to indemnify. This insurance does not cover criminal or dishonest acts, events from which the insider obtained personal gain, or circumstances in which a conflict of interest was apparent.

Financial institutions whose securities are listed on the national exchanges may have additional requirements regarding the adoption and disclosure of compensation guidelines.

Many banks may rely on incentive pay to attract, motivate, and retain insiders. However, incentive-based compensation arrangements that provide incentives contrary to the safe and sound operation of the institution should be avoided. It is the board's responsibility to review and closely monitor all insider incentives to ensure that they do not result in any unreasonable risk-taking to the bank.

Management and Other Fees

Fees paid to insiders for services rendered to, or on behalf of, the bank must be for services that meet the legitimate needs of the bank, must be justified, and must be reasonable in amount. The OCC considers fees reasonable if they are based on fair market cost, or fair market cost plus a fair profit. Reasonable costs may include overhead expenses to the extent they are a legitimate and integral part of the services provided. Debt service requirements of a parent company or other shareholders do not represent a legitimate overhead expense that may be imposed upon or allocated to a national bank.

Banks that pay management or other fees to insiders should retain well-documented records that demonstrate the fair value of the goods and services received, their benefit to the bank, and the appropriateness of the fees paid. These records should be reviewed by the board of directors as part of its ongoing oversight of the bank's affairs.

If excessive management or other fees are paid to insiders, the board of directors is responsible for taking corrective action, possibly to include making restitution. Further, if the payment of excessive fees results in the levy of additional income taxes, the recipient and the members of the board of directors that approved the fees may be responsible for paying those taxes.

Prepayment of fees by a bank for services not yet received may constitute a violation of section 23B of the Federal Reserve Act (12 USC 371c-1), if the insider is also an "affiliate" under section 23B.

Audit Committee Member Fees

Audit committee members of public banks or bank holding companies[7] are barred from accepting any consulting, advisory, or other compensatory fee, other than director and board committee fees.[8]

Credit Life/Accident and Health Insurance Fees

12 CFR 2 provides that it is an unsafe and unsound practice for any bank insider who is involved in the sale of credit life, accident, or health insurance to lend money to customers of the bank to purchase such insurance when the

---

[7] Public banks and bank holding companies are defined as those that have securities registered with the OCC or SEC.

[8] However, based on the specific circumstances, audit committee members may or may not be prohibited from engaging in other business with the bank. See Section 301 of the Sarbanes-Oxley Act, as well as the "Management and Board Supervision" booklet of the *Comptroller's Handbook* for additional discussion of this issue.

insider profits from the sale. It also prohibits insiders, and any entities controlled by such persons, from retaining commissions or other income from the sale of such insurance, to loan customers. In addition, it sets forth guidance for bonus and incentive plans based on the sale of credit life insurance.

Other Commissions or Fees Paid to Insiders

The payment to insiders of commissions or fees derived from services they or their related interests provide to bank customers could create a conflict of interest if they are either directly or indirectly involved in the approval of a loan or other transaction at the bank for which they are receiving the commissions or fees. Such services may include the sale of title insurance, the sale of hazard insurance relating to bank collateral, legal and/or appraisal services, etc. Insiders who receive payment of commissions or fees directly or indirectly related to a loan or other bank transaction in which they have an interest should fully disclose their interest and abstain from participating in the approval of that transaction.

Dividends

The board of directors should ensure that any proposed dividend is consistent with the bank's capital and strategic plans and will not have an adverse impact on capital adequacy. The dividend policies of a national bank should be consistent with its capacity to pay and should not be based in any way on the needs of insiders or shareholders. Dividend policies based solely on insiders' or their interests' need for income are considered unsafe and unsound. If a dividend in excess of the limit imposed by 12 USC 60(b) is contemplated, the bank should request permission from the OCC, in advance, to pay the dividend.

Management Information Systems and Financial Reporting

Banks should have sound information systems that produce the information necessary to assess compliance with insider laws, regulations, and policies. The information gathered through these systems should fully support regulatory and board reporting. In addition, the systems should aggregate extensions of credit to insiders and their related interests to help maintain compliance with statutory limitations.

Proper record keeping is essential for the board and management to effectively monitor insider relationships and lending and to file accurate call reports. Schedule RC-M of the call report requires banks to report extensions of credit to executive officers, directors, principal shareholders, and their related interests. In addition, each bank must furnish a report of all loans or extensions of credit it has made to executive officers since the previous call report date.

National banks registered with the OCC and national bank holding companies that have securities registered with the SEC are also subject to accelerated reporting of insider securities transactions. Registered banks or bank holding companies must file reports with the appropriate federal banking regulator within two business days following the date on which the insider transaction was executed. Institutions with Web sites are also required to disclose the reports on the Web sites.

OCC Evaluation of Insider Activities

OCC examiners will focus on the adequacy of the bank's policies governing insider activities and the processes for monitoring compliance with these policies and applicable law. Examiners will determine whether the bank's internal controls and management information systems are adequate and protect the bank against insider abuse. In addition, examiners should assess the cause of any deficiencies and request appropriate corrective action from management and the board.

Examiners will complete, when appropriate, community or large bank management core assessment procedures, located respectively in the "Community Bank Supervision" and "Large Bank Supervision" booklets of the *Comptroller's Handbook*, during the course of a bank's supervisory cycle. Core assessment standards are the minimum procedures that must be performed to reach conclusions about the condition of each bank. These procedures are conducted through either the on-site examination process or through other supervisory activities, such as ongoing monitoring and director and management meetings.

Examiners should supplement, as necessary, the core assessment procedures with the insider activities procedures in this booklet. The extent to which an examiner uses all or some of these supplemental procedures should reflect the bank's history of insider violations, if there are indications of significant changes in insiders or insider activity, if the bank's internal policies and risk management system show signs of inadequacy, and if the management team is inexperienced or its background is otherwise questionable.

In reviewing payments to insiders for goods or services (including fees the bank pays to insiders, payments by the bank's customers to insiders for work on the bank's behalf as well as third party loan proceeds used to purchase goods or services from insiders), examiners should not establish pricing criteria. However, they should be alert to situations when costs of such goods and services are not in accord with market rates, are arbitrarily inflated, are inflated because of inefficiencies, or exceed the cost of acquiring the same services elsewhere. The board and management should have systems and controls in place to prevent inappropriate or unreasonable fees or other payments to insiders.

Examiners should thoroughly discuss examination findings and inappropriate insider transactions with bank management and the board of directors. Bank management should correct violations of insider requirements immediately. Whenever a violation occurs, and particularly whenever a violation continues from one examination to the next, it may indicate poor management and inadequate board oversight. The examiner should always clearly communicate the findings of any violations, the need for corrective action, and the time frame for such action in the "Matters Requiring Attention" and "Violations" sections of the report of examination. Further, the examiner should decide whether enforcement action against the bank and the persons who approved or benefited from the transactions is warranted.

For additional information and guidance regarding potential insider loan abuse, examiners may refer to the FFIEC White Paper, "The Detection, Investigation, and Prevention of Insider Loan Fraud," May 2003, available at www.ffiec.gov/exam/whitepapers.htm.

The detailed procedures in this booklet are designed to help examiners reach a conclusion about a bank's insider activities. This conclusion should reflect insider activity findings from several targeted reviews throughout the bank or from a centralized insider activity evaluation.

Examination Procedures

General Procedures

Many of the steps in these examination procedures require gathering information from, or reviewing information with, examiners in other areas of the examination. Since many other areas include examination procedures that address insider concerns, discussing this review with the examiners who evaluated those areas can reduce burden on the bank and avoid duplication of effort. By sharing examination data, examiners also can cross check compliance effectively and assess more readily the integrity of management information systems.

Information from other areas should be cross-referenced in the working papers as appropriate. Specific examination information that is not available from other examiners should be requested from the bank. However, the final decision regarding the scope of the examination and how best to obtain needed information rests with the examiner-in-charge.

Objective: To set the scope for the review of insider activities.

1. Obtain the following information:

    •   The examination scope memorandum issued by the examiner-in-charge.
    •   The most recent examination reports, including any reports issued by other regulators, as available.
    •   Written insider policies, including a code of ethics.
    •   Internal/external audit reports.
    •   Reports in the OCC databases (e.g., UBPR).
    •   Other internal bank reports.

2. Determine any material changes since the previous examination. Examples include:

    •   New executive officers.
    •   New directors.
    •   New affiliations or related interests by directors and/or management.
    •   Ownership changes.

3. Review, as appropriate, OCC databases, the previous examination report, examination reports of other regulators, internal/external audit reports, internal bank reports, and any trust examination report for information about conflicts of interest or insider abuse. Pertinent information may surface in the following examination areas:

- Analytical review of income and expense.
- Bank dealer activities.
- Compliance management.
- Deposit accounts.
- Duties and responsibilities of directors.
- Ownership records.
- Trust department activities.
- International banking.
- Investment securities.
- Loan portfolio management.
- Private placements.

4. Based on the performance of the previous steps and discussions with the bank EIC and other appropriate supervisors, determine the scope and set the objectives for this examination.

Quantity of Risk

Conclusion: The quantity of risk is (low, moderate, high).

Conclusion: The bank (is/is not) in compliance with laws and regulations governing insider activities.

Objective: To determine the bank's vulnerability to insider abuse and its level of compliance with established laws, regulations, and policies regarding insider transactions and activities.

1. Obtain the following documents or, if appropriate, review the information with the examiner assigned to the relevant area:

    *   Board of directors' minutes containing insider transaction information, including any potential or existing conflicts of interest.
    *   A list of executive officers, including
        – Name.
        – Title.
        – Date the person became an executive officer.
        – Related interests.
    *   A list of directors, including:
        – Name.
        – Date the director was elected to the board.
        – Related interests.
    *   A list of shareholders with more than 10 percent ownership, including:
        – Shareholder name.
        – Date the person became a principal shareholder.
        – Number of shares owned.
        – Related interests.
    *   A list of extensions of credit (including commitments) to directors, executive officers, principal shareholders, and their related interests, describing:
        – Complete name of obligor, co-maker, endorser, and guarantor.
        – Type of entity (individual, sole proprietorship, general partnership, limited partnership, limited liability company, corporation).
        – Name of director, officer, or principal shareholder related to the obligor.

- Nature of obligation (signer on note, guarantor, general partner, etc.)
- Original date, amount, and purpose of the loan or commitment.
- Current balance.
- Terms, including interest rate, maturity date, and any collateral.
- Status (delinquent, restructured, renegotiated, or considered a problem loan by management).
- Date reported to, or approved by, the board of directors, if applicable.

- A copy of the Report of Indebtedness of Executive Officers and Principal Shareholders and Their Related Interests to Correspondent Banks (FFIEC Form 004) or similar form containing identical information, if applicable.
- A report of executive officer borrowings at other institutions required by 12 CFR 215.9, if applicable.
- Any bank-generated overdraft report to ensure compliance with 12 CFR 215.4(e)(1).
- A list of deposit accounts and other vehicles not technically deposits (e.g., repurchase agreements) of directors, officers, and all other employees to ensure that they are not receiving preferential interest rates (12 USC 376).
- A list of comparable non-insider transactions.
- A report of fees or other payments made as well as any reimbursements of personal expenses (e.g., consulting or other professional services) paid to insiders and their related interests.
- A list of management officials (as defined in 12 USC 3201) of the bank, its holding company, and holding company affiliates, who are management officials of other depository institutions.
- A list of purchases or sales of assets to, or use of bank property by, an insider.
- A list of loans to third parties of which the proceeds were either directly or indirectly transferred to a bank insider or used for the tangible economic benefit of a bank insider.

2. From the materials gathered above, select a representative sample of insider borrowings. Review terms of extensions of credit (including renewals), such as interest rates, fees charged, and collateral. Assess compliance with laws and regulations for loans to insiders by determining whether these extensions of credit and loan renewals:

- Are made on substantially the same terms and adhere to credit underwriting practices that are no less stringent than those available at the same time to non-insiders for comparable transactions (12 USC 375a(1) and 375b(2) and 12 CFR 215.4(a)(1).

- Are made pursuant to an employee benefit or compensation plan which is widely available to employees (12 CFR 215.4(a)(2)).
- Carry no more than a normal risk of failure to repay (12 USC 375a(1) and 375b(2) and 12 CFR 215.4(a)(1)).
- Have no other unfavorable features (12 USC 375a(1), 12 USC 375b(2), and 12 CFR 215.4(a)(1)).
- Do not exceed the greater of $25,000 or 5 percent of the bank's unimpaired capital and unimpaired surplus (12 USC 375b(3) and 12 CFR 215.4(b)). If loans exceed these limits, determine whether:
  - The extension of credit was approved in advance by a disinterested majority of the entire board of directors (12 USC 375b(3)(A) and 12 CFR 31.2(a) and 215.4(b)(1)(i)).
  - The interested party abstained from participating directly or indirectly in the deliberations and voting (12 USC 375b(3)(B) and 12 CFR 31.2(a), 215.4(b)(1)(ii) and 215.4(b)(4)).
  - The abstention was noted in the board of directors' minutes. (Although this is not required by regulation, the OCC believes this is a prudent banking practice.)
  - There is prior approval for any aggregate extension of credit to the insider and all related interests of the insider exceeding $500,000 (12 USC 375b(3) and 12 CFR 215.4(b)(2) and (3)).

3.   Using bank reports and other materials gathered, determine whether aggregate loans to any individual and related interests exceed the limit on loans to a single borrower established by 12 USC 84 (which includes any higher limits permitted by section 84, 12 USC 375b(4), and 12 CFR 215.4(c)).

4.   Using bank reports and other materials gathered, determine whether aggregate extensions of credit to executive officers, directors, and principal shareholders and their related interests exceed the bank's unimpaired capital and unimpaired surplus. If loans exceed that limit, determine whether the bank has total deposits of less than $100 million (12 USC 375b(5)(A) and 12 CFR 215.4(d)(1)). If the bank has total deposits of less than $100 million, determine whether:

- Total extensions to insiders do not exceed two times the bank's unimpaired capital and unimpaired surplus (12 CFR 215.4(d)(2)).

- The board determined the higher limit is consistent with safe and sound banking practices and is necessary to attract or retain directors or prevent restricting credit availability in small communities (12 USC 375b(5)(C) and 12 CFR 215.4(d)(2)(i)(A)).
- The board's annual resolution sets forth the facts and reasoning of the resolution, including the amount of the bank's lending to its insiders as a percentage of the bank's unimpaired capital and unimpaired surplus as of the date of the resolution (12 CFR 215.4(d)(2)(i)(B)).
- The bank meets or exceeds all applicable capital requirements (12 CFR 3, 12 CFR 215.4(d)(2)(i)(C)).
- The bank received at least a satisfactory composite rating on its most recent examination (12 CFR 215.4(d)(2)(i)(D)).
- If the bank subsequently failed to qualify for the higher limit, it did not extend additional credit that would maintain insider lending in excess of 100 percent of unimpaired capital and surplus (12 CFR 215.4(d)(2)(ii)).
- Any exceptions are consistent with the requirements in 12 CFR 215.4(d)(3).

5. Determine whether the proceeds of any loans to third parties were transferred to, or used for the benefit of, any insider and, if so, whether such transfer or benefit qualifies for an exception to the "tangible, economic benefit" rule. (12 CFR 215.3(f))

6. With respect to principal shareholders, determine whether any loans were made to members of that shareholder's "immediate family," as that term is defined in 12 CFR 215.2(g).

7. Determine whether any executive officer, director, or principal shareholder knowingly received or knowingly permitted any of that person's related interests to receive from any member bank, directly or indirectly, an extension of credit (as defined in 12 CFR 215.3) not authorized by 12 USC 375a, 375b or Regulation O (12 CFR 215.6).

8. Determine whether a mortgage or a home equity loan to an executive officer:

- Is to finance or refinance the purchase, construction, maintenance, or improvement of a residence of the executive officer (12 USC 375a(2)(A) and 12 CFR 215.5(c)(2)).

- Is secured by a first lien on the residence the executive officer owns or expects to own after the extension of credit (12 USC 375a(2)(A) and 12 CFR 215.5(c)(2)(i)).
- Is a refinancing and, if so, whether the amount used to repay the original extension of credit, together with closing costs and any other additional amount used, reflect permissible purposes (12 CFR 215.5(c)(2)(ii)).
- Is the **only** such loan outstanding (12 USC 375a(2)(B)).

9. Determine whether loans to any executive officer for purposes other than first-lien mortgages or children's educations, at any one time, do not aggregate to more than $25,000 or 2.5 percent of the bank's unimpaired capital and unimpaired surplus (limited to $100,000), whichever is greater (12 USC 375a(4) and 12 CFR 31.2(a) and 215.5(c)(4)).

10. Determine whether exceptions to the limits outlined in 12 CFR 215.4(d)(1) are secured, consistent with 12 CFR 31.2(a) and 12 CFR 215.4(d)(3).

11. Determine whether extensions of credit to executive officers are:

- Promptly reported to the board of directors (12 USC 375a(1) and 12 CFR 215.5(d)(1)).
- Made on substantially the same terms as, and adhere to credit underwriting practices that are no less stringent than, those prevailing at the time for other persons (12 USC 375a(1)(B) and 12 CFR 215.4(a) and 215.5(d)(2)).
- Preceded by the submission of a detailed current financial statement of the executive officer (12 USC 375a(1)(C) and 12 CFR 215.5(d)(3)).
- Made under the written condition that the extension of credit shall become due and payable on demand at any time that the officer is indebted to any other bank(s) in an aggregate amount greater than the amount specified for a category of credit in section 215.5(c), 12 USC 375a(1)(D) and 12 CFR 215.5(d)(4)).

12. Determine whether bank records on insider borrowings satisfy the record keeping requirements of 12 CFR 215.8, including:

- Identifying all insiders of the bank and their related interests, annually (12 CFR 215.8(b)(1)).

- Specifying the amount and terms of each extension of credit to insiders of the bank (12 CFR 215.8(b)(2)).
- Maintaining records of extensions of credit to insiders of the bank's affiliates using one of the methods specified in 12 CFR 215.8(c).
- Employing a record keeping method the OCC determines is effective (12 CFR 215.8(c)(3)).

13. Determine whether executive officers and principal shareholders have made written reports to the board of directors of their bank on borrowings from other banks (12 USC 375a(6) and 1972(2)(G)(i) and 12 CFR 215.9 and 215.22(a)) in sufficient detail to determine the existence of any quid pro quo arrangements, including:

- Reports, made within 10 days, of indebtedness to other banks in an aggregate amount greater than they could borrow from their own bank (12 CFR 215.9).
- Reports of indebtedness of the executive officer or principal shareholder and their related interests outstanding to each correspondent bank (12 CFR 215.22(b)(2)).

14. Determine whether the bank's most recently filed call report included:

- A report of all extensions of credit made by the bank to its executive officers since the previous call report. Coordinate your efforts with the examiners reviewing regulatory reports and loan portfolio management to avoid duplication (12 USC 375a(9) and 12 CFR 215.10)).
- An accurate reporting of extensions of credit to executive officers, directors, principal shareholders and their related interests (12 USC 161 and 1817(a)(3) and 12 CFR 215.10).

15. Determine whether, upon written request from the public, the bank makes available the names of insiders to whom the bank had extended credit, aggregate extensions of credit, and other required information (12 CFR 215.11(b)).

16. Determine whether each executive officer and director of a national bank that is not publicly traded reports the outstanding amount of any credit extended to him or her based on the security of shares of the bank, to the board of directors annually (12 CFR 215.12).

17. Using bank reports and other materials, determine whether all loans by the bank to insiders of its correspondent banks:

   - Are on terms no more favorable than those available at the same time to non-insiders for comparable transactions (12 USC 1972(2)).
   - Carry no more than the normal risk of failure to repay (12 USC 1972(2)).
   - Have no other unfavorable features (12 USC 1972(2)).

18. Review purchases and sales of securities and other property to or from directors or to a director's firm and determine whether they are on terms that are no less favorable to the bank than those available to other parties or, alternatively, whether the bank's board of directors has approved the sale or purchase (12 USC 375).

19. Review fees paid to insiders and determine whether they have a direct relationship to, and are based solely upon, the fair value of goods and services received and compensate the insider only for providing goods and services that meet the legitimate needs of the bank (and do not place the insider in a conflict of interest relative to his or her duties at the bank).

20. Review a sample of deposit accounts of executive officers, directors, principal shareholders, and their related interests and identify any:

   - Exceptions to standard policies on service charges and interest paid.
   - Self-dealing or preferential treatment (12 USC 376).
   - Cash items being held by the bank to prevent an overdraft (12 USC 375b(6) and 12 CFR 215.3(b)(2)).
   - Overdrafts being paid for executive officers and/or directors on an account at the bank (12 USC 375b(6) and 12 CFR 215.4(e)). For any such overdrafts, determine whether the overdraft:
     - Was in accordance with a written, pre-authorized interest-bearing extension-of-credit plan that specifies a method of repayment (12 USC 375b(6)(B)(i) and 12 CFR 215.4(e)(1)(i)); or
     - Was in accordance with a written, pre-authorized transfer of funds from another account of the account holder at the bank (12 USC 375b(6)(B)(ii) and 12 CFR 215.4(e)(1)(ii)); or
     - Was inadvertent, and aggregated $1,000 or less (12 CFR 215.4(e)(2)). If overdrafts were inadvertent, determine whether

the overdraft status continued no more than five business days and the executive officer or director paid the same fee charged any other customer of the bank in similar circumstances (12 CFR 215.4(e)(2)(i) and (ii)).

Note that in steps 2 through 20, any violation of Regulation O (12 CFR 215) will also be a violation of 12 CFR 31.2(a), Extensions of Credit to Insiders and Transactions with Affiliates.

21. Determine, through discussion with the examiner assigned insurance, whether directors and officers liability insurance is in effect. If so:

    - Determine whether any reviews have been performed of the insider area.
    - Determine whether insurance policies include any insider exclusions.

22. If the bank sells credit life, or accident and health insurance, prepare a description of the program(s), including:

    - A list of insiders who are licensed insurance agents.
    - Any bonus or incentive compensation programs.
    - The disposition of commission payments.

23. For banks that sell credit life or accident and health insurance, test for compliance with 12 CFR 2. Determine that:

    - The bank has not structured its bonus or incentive plan in a manner that could create incentives for persons selling credit life insurance to make inappropriate recommendations or sales of credit life insurance to bank customers (12 CFR 2.3(b)).
    - In any bonus or incentive plan for bank employees or officers based on credit life insurance sales (12 CFR 2.4(a)),
      - Payments are in amounts that do not exceed 5 percent of the recipient's annual salary; or
      - Payments to any one individual during a year do not exceed 5 percent of the average salary of all loan officers participating in the plan.
    - Income is not being improperly retained by an employee, officer, director, or principal shareholder, or by an entity in which such persons have more than a 10 percent interest (12 CFR 2.3(c)).

- When an affiliate receives credit life insurance income, the bank is properly reimbursed for the use of its premises, personnel, and goodwill and that reimbursement is equal to at least 20 percent of the affiliate's net income attributable to the bank's credit life insurance sales (12 CFR 2.5(b)).

24. If insiders receive payment of commissions or fees from the bank derived from services they or their related interests provide to bank customers, determine whether:

- The insider is directly or indirectly involved in the approval of a loan or other transaction at the bank for which they are receiving the commission or fees.
- Insiders who receive payment of commissions or fees directly or indirectly related to a loan or other bank transaction in which they have an interest have fully disclosed their interest and abstained from participating in the approval or that transaction.

25. Determine whether any management official of the bank or its holding company or affiliates of the holding company is also a management official of an unaffiliated depository institution or depository institution holding company and evaluate whether the relationship complies with the Depository Institution Management Interlocks Act (12 USC 3201 and 12 CFR 26).

26. Determine whether the purchase or sale of assets to insiders and their related interests was reported to the board and the bank obtained an independent appraisal of the asset.

27. Determine whether the use of bank property by insiders and their related interests was reported to the board, a determination was made as to reasonableness of ownership, tax implications were evaluated, and the bank's tax accountant was consulted with regard to the use of the property and is in compliance with bank policy.

28. Determine whether any payments to insiders have been reported to the board and an independent assessment of the value of services have been performed in relation to the bank's need for them.

29. Determine whether reimbursement of personal expenses to insiders is of

a legitimate nature, is legal, is reasonable, and, when necessary, is reported to the board. Examiners should consider testing vouchers and reimbursable/payable transactions if controls are weak, and should consider tracing loan funds if suspicious loans or activities are identified.

Quality of Risk Management

Conclusion: The quality of risk management is (strong, satisfactory, weak).

Policy

Conclusion: The board (has, has not) established adequate policies to ensure compliance with laws and regulations as well as arm's length transactions regarding insider activities.

Objective: To determine whether the bank's written insider policies adequately address both the existence and appearance of conflicts of interest and breaches of fiduciary duty.

1.   Review the insider policies for procedures governing:

- Disclosure to the board of actual or potential conflicts of interest.
- Abstention by insiders from the approval process on any transaction in which the insider may benefit directly or indirectly from the decision.
- Officers who may enter into insider transactions on the bank's behalf.

2.   Determine whether the policies appropriately address disclosures by insiders:

- Of any interest in the business of a borrower or other bank customer.
- Of any interest in the companies who are supplying goods or services to the bank or doing business on behalf of the bank.
- Of transactions with the bank including payment to or receipt from the bank of fees or commissions.
- Of other related interests as required in 12 CFR 215.

3.   Determine whether the policies clearly communicate the circumstances and conditions under which:

- The bank may enter into transactions with insiders or their related interests.

- The bank will make the use of its facilities, real or personal property, or personnel available to insiders.

4. Assess whether the policies adequately address prohibitions that preclude insiders from:

    - Soliciting anything of value from anyone in return for any business service or confidential information of the bank.
    - Accepting anything of value other than their bona fide salary, wages, fees, or other compensation paid in the usual course of business by their employer, from anyone in connection with the business of the bank, either before or after a transaction is discussed or consummated.
    - Accepting gifts, bequests, or other items of value from bank customers or other persons with business dealings with the bank.
    - Using insider information in securities transactions.

5. Review policy requirements for arm's length transactions:

    - With insiders or their related interests.
    - With businesses with which the bank deals if the business is one in which an insider has an interest.

6. Determine whether the policies adequately address the consequences of breaches of fiduciary duty, unethical conduct, violations of law, or suspected criminal activity, and contain effective internal reporting mechanisms as well as SAR filing processes.

7. Review policy requirements for documentation of insider transactions.

8. Determine whether the bank periodically reviews its insider policies to ensure that they reflect any changes in laws or regulations. Determine whether:

    - Insiders have copies of the document and have signed an acknowledgement form.
    - Insiders are advised of their responsibilities.
    - The bank provides training updates.

Processes

Conclusion: Internal operating procedures and information systems (are, are not) effective in enabling management to comply with laws and regulations as well as avoiding even the appearance of preferential treatment regarding insider activities.

Objective: To ensure that the bank's operating procedures and information systems are adequate to enable management to comply with laws and regulations and board-established policies regarding insider activities.

1. Review bank management information systems, and determine whether they:

   - Can provide aggregate data on insiders and their related interests.
   - Can ensure proper monitoring of, and compliance with, insider lending restrictions (see 12 CFR 215.8 for record keeping requirements).
   - Require that reports on insiders be retained for at least three years (12 CFR 215.22(d)).
   - Require that records of publicly requested disclosures of information be retained for two years from the date of the request (12 CFR 31.2(a) and 215.23(b)).

2. Determine whether the bank has established communication channels outside the normal chain of command through which employees can seek advice on ethics or compliance questions.

3. Determine whether the bank's employment practices include performing periodic background checks on insiders.

4. Determine whether insider-related reports are being reviewed by management and the board.

Personnel

Conclusion: Bank personnel (are, are not) aware of regulatory requirements regarding insider activities.

Objective: To ensure that bank personnel are aware of the requirements of laws and regulations as well as the importance of avoiding even the appearance of impropriety regarding insider activities.

1. Determine through discussion with compliance and audit personnel their knowledge with regard to laws and regulations addressing insider activities. Review:

    • Scope of the compliance or audit review program.
    • Compliance or audit review findings.

2. Determine whether management ensures personnel are aware of regulatory requirements regarding insider activities.

    • Has the bank notified each of its executive officers and directors of the reporting requirements of 12 CFR 31.2(a) and 215.22(e)?
    • Has the bank established an ongoing program to educate and raise the awareness of all bank employees regarding its insider policies?
    • Has the bank established a confidential process by which personnel may bring potential conflicts of interest or improper situations to the attention of management and the board?
    • Has management provided training to personnel regarding regulatory and bank-established policy requirements, including training for regulatory and policy changes/updates, at least annually?
    • Do the bank's written insider policies require affected personnel to acknowledge reading the policy, including updates, and abiding by their terms?

Control Systems

Conclusion: Control systems (are, are not) effective.

Objective: To ensure that the board has established effective control systems that enable management to comply with laws, regulations, and policies as well as safe and sound banking practices regarding insider activities. These controls should be set up in such a manner as to also be effective in preventing anyone from overriding them.

1. Review the internal and external audit, compliance, and/or internal loan

review functions and working papers as they relate to existing and proposed insider transactions. Determine whether:

- Their function is adequate in terms of:
  - Independence.
  - Scope (e.g., testing for compliance with laws and regulations).
  - Coverage (e.g., includes review of income received from and fees paid to insiders and their related interests).
  - Frequency of review.
  - Procedures.
- Bank management and the board of directors take timely corrective action to address deficiencies noted by the audit, compliance, and/or internal loan review functions.

2. Does the bank, through the audit department or other independent source, review and report to the board of directors or committee:

- Existing transactions between insiders for compliance with the bank's conflicts of interest policy?
- Proposed transactions, or modifications of existing relationships, between the bank and any of its insiders and their interests?
- Insider transactions for compliance with laws, rules, and regulations including breaches of fiduciary duty or unethical conduct?
- Testing performed to ensure the completeness and accuracy of insider reporting?
- Whether the bank accurately calculates unimpaired capital and unimpaired surplus for Regulation O purposes? (This should be done in conjunction with the examiner reviewing capital.)

3. Has a process been implemented to prevent anyone from overriding the control systems, and are the systems checked periodically to ensure that they have not been compromised by anyone? Has the system been tested?

Conclusion Procedures

Objective: To communicate examination findings and initiate appropriate corrective action.

1.   Provide the EIC with conclusion of findings, focusing on:

   - The bank's policies, management information systems, controls, and their impact on the bank's capacity to operate in a safe and sound manner.
   - Compliance with established laws, rules, and regulations.
   - The quality and effectiveness of the bank's insider policies and procedures and the bank's vulnerability to insider abuse.
   - The adequacy of audit coverage of insider activities.
   - Any corrective action needed for deficient policies, practices, procedures, internal controls, or violations of law. In determining appropriate corrective action, consider whether deficiencies:

      - Reflect a lax attitude or lack of understanding of insider issues by management.
      - Resulted from bank personnel's lack of familiarity with the laws, rulings, and regulations, or bank-established policy.
      - Reflect a failure by bank management to implement corrective action for deficiencies cited at previous bank or regulatory reviews.
      - Resulted from specific weaknesses in the bank's systems.
      - Are technical and not expected to recur because adequate systems exist.

2.   Determine the impact on aggregate risk and the direction of risk assessments for any risks identified when performing the above procedures. Examiners should refer to guidance provided under the OCC's large and community bank risk assessment programs.

   - Risk Categories: Compliance, Credit, Reputation, Strategic
   - Risk Conclusions: High, Moderate, or Low
   - Risk Direction: Increasing, Stable, or Declining

3.   Determine, in consultation with the EIC, whether the risks identified are

significant enough to merit bringing them to the board's attention in the report of examination. If so, prepare items for inclusion under the heading Matters Requiring Attention (MRA). Use the following guidelines when preparing these items:

- An MRA is a bank practice that:
  - Deviates from sound fundamental governance, internal control, and risk management principles, which may adversely impact the bank's earnings or capital, risk profile, or reputation if not addressed.
  - Results in substantive noncompliance with laws or internal policies or processes.
- While there is no specific format for MRAs, when composing an MRA you should provide the following details:
  - Description of MRA;
  - Factors contributing to the problem, including its root cause;
  - Consequences of inaction;
  - Management's commitment to corrective action; and
  - The time frame for corrective action and the person(s) responsible for taking such action.

4. Determine in consultation with appropriate OCC personnel whether any enforcement action should be recommended (e.g., formal agreement, cease and desist order, civil money penalty) or a Suspicious Activity Report should be filed.

5. Discuss findings with management, including:

- Overall conclusions, specifically regarding applicable risks.
- Violations of law or regulation and non-conformance with bank policy.
- Deficiencies.
- Recommendations.
- If applicable, commitment from management to correct violations of law and/or Matters Requiring Attention.

6. As appropriate, prepare an insider activities comment for inclusion in the Report of Examination.

7. Advise appropriate OCC offices of any insider borrowings in this institution that may affect insiders in another national bank (12 USC

1972(2)). Also advise the district office of similar situations that may affect state banks.

8. Update the OCC supervisory database and any applicable Report of Examination schedules or tables. When appropriate, add information regarding insider borrowings at other banks.

9. Organize and reference working papers in accordance with OCC guidance. Prepare a memorandum or update the work program with any information that will facilitate future examinations.

Appendix A
General Rules on Insider Lending

This chart is a general guide to the statutes and regulations governing loans to insiders. It does not cover all aspects of the laws and regulations.

Affected Parties	12 USC 375a	12 USC 375b	12 CFR 215
Executive officers, directors, principal shareholders, and related interests	Applies only to executive officers.	Prohibits preferential terms, higher-than-normal risk of repayment, other unfavorable features. Loans to the person are combined with loans to related interests of the person for purposes of borrowing limits. The borrowing amount is subject to the single-borrower limits under 12 USC 84. Aggregate of all extensions of credit to insiders is limited to 100 percent of unimpaired capital and unimpaired surplus. Limit may be doubled for adequately capitalized banks with deposits of less than $100 million. Prohibits receiving an extension of credit not authorized under this section. Prohibits overdrafts unless pursuant to a preauthorized written agreement (executive officers and directors only).	Prohibits preferential terms, higher-than-normal risk of repayment, other unfavorable features. Loans to the person are combined with loans to related interests of the person for purposes of borrowing limits. Prior board approval, with the interested party abstaining, is required for an extension of credit to the person in an amount that, when aggregated with all other extensions of credit to the person and the related interests of the person, exceeds the greater of $25,000 or 5 percent of capital and surplus, and in all cases for an extension of credit to the person in an amount that, when aggregated with all other extensions of credit to the person and the related interests of the person, exceeds $500,000. The borrowing amount is subject to the single-borrower limits under 12 USC 84. Aggregate of all extensions of credit to insiders is limited to 100 percent of unimpaired capital and unimpaired surplus, with certain exceptions based on the nature of collateral. Overdrafts of *executive officers and directors* may not be paid except subject to certain conditions, unless the overdrawn account is $1,000 or less, the account is overdrawn for no more than five business days, and the insider is charged the same fee as any other customer in similar circumstances.

Affected Parties	12 USC 375a	12 USC 375b	12 CFR 215
Executive officers only	Imposes additional limits on a bank's extensions of credit to executive officers, including requirements that the loans be at arm's length and preceded by the submission of a financial statement. Allows 1st lien mortgage loans and loans to finance children's education without limit (although 375b imposes aggregate limits).		"Other purpose" loans are limited by 12 CFR 215.5 to $25,000 or 2.5 percent of unimpaired capital and unimpaired surplus, whichever is greater, up to $100,000.

Appendix B

Regulation O Reporting Requirements

The following is an aid to understanding the various reporting requirements for insider transactions. It is only a guide and cannot substitute for reading and studying 12 USC 375, 375a, 375b, and 1972 and 12 CFR 31 and 215 (Regulation O).

Definitions

An "executive officer" is a person who participates (other than in the capacity of a director) or who has the authority to participate in major policy-making functions whether or not the person has an official title (12 CFR 215.2(e)(1)). Persons holding certain titles are presumed to be "executive officers" unless properly excluded by the bank's board of directors in accordance with Regulation O's specified procedures and they do not actually engage in major policy-making functions of the bank. In addition, for all purposes except 12 CFR 215.5, an "executive officer" includes an executive officer of a company or any subsidiary of a company of which the member bank is a subsidiary. Regulation O permits a bank's board of directors to exclude officers of affiliates if certain procedural and substantive requirements are met (12 CFR 215.2(e)(2)). Officers of bank subsidiaries are generally not considered "executive officers" of their parent bank unless they actually engage in major policy-making functions *of the bank.*

A "principal shareholder" is a natural person (not a company of which the bank is a subsidiary) who directly or indirectly, or acting through or in concert with one or more persons, owns, controls, or has the power to vote more than 10 percent of any class of voting securities. Shares owned or controlled by a member of an individual's immediate family are considered as being held by the individual (12 CFR 215.2(m)).

A "related interest" of a person is (1) a company controlled by that person; or (2) a political or campaign committee that is controlled by that person, the funds or services of which will benefit that person (12 CFR 215.2(n)).

Summary of Requirements

Section   Requirement

215.8 Records of Member Banks
The bank must maintain records that identify each insider of the bank by conducting an annual survey. Alternative methods are permitted for identifying insiders of the bank's affiliates. The bank must also specify the amount and terms of each extension of credit made to any insider.

215.9 Reports by Executive Officers
Executive officers must provide a written report to the board of directors within 10 days of becoming indebted to any other bank or banks if the aggregate amount of the indebtedness exceeds $100,000 (or the greater of 2.5 percent of the bank's capital and surplus or $25,000), subject to the exceptions in section 215.5(c). The report shall state the lender's name and the date, amount, security, and purpose for each extension of credit.

215.10 Reports on Credit to Executive Officers
Banks must include with the call report a report of all extensions of credit to executive officers since the previous call report.

215.11 Disclosure of Credit From Member Banks to Executive Officers and Principal Shareholders
Upon written request from the public, the bank shall make available the names of its executive officers and principal shareholders to whom, or to whose related interests, the bank has outstanding as of the last quarter-end an extension of credit that, when aggregated with all other extensions of credit to that person and the related interests of that person, equals or exceeds 5 percent of unimpaired capital and unimpaired surplus, or $500,000, whichever is less. Records of such requests must be maintained for two years.

215.12 Reporting Requirement for Credit Secured by Certain Bank Stock
Executive officers or directors of the bank whose shares are not publicly traded must annually report to the board their outstanding amount of any credit secured by shares of the bank.

215.22 Reports by Executive Officers and Principal Shareholders or their Related Interests

Annually, on or before January 31, executive officers and principal shareholders must report to the board of directors the (1) maximum indebtedness of the executive officer and principal shareholder and of each of that person's related interests to each correspondent bank during the previous year, and (2) the amount of indebtedness of the executive officer or principal shareholder and of each of that person's related interests to each correspondent bank as of 10 business days before the required January 31 filing date. The report must include a description of the terms and conditions of each extension of credit included in the indebtedness reported. The bank must notify executive officers and principal shareholders of this requirement, make available a list of correspondent banks, and maintain the reports for three years. Banks may use FFIEC Form 004 or maintain the information in a similar format.

215.23 Disclosure of Credit from Correspondent Banks to Executive Officers and Principal Shareholders

Upon written request from the public, the bank shall make available the names of executive officers and principal shareholders to whom, or to whose related interests, any correspondent bank had outstanding at any time during the previous year an extension of credit that, when aggregated with all other extensions of credit at such time from all correspondent banks to that person and the related interests of that person, equals or exceeds 5 percent of unimpaired capital and unimpaired surplus or $500,000, whichever is less. Records of such requests must be maintained for two years.

Appendix C

Other Insider Laws and Regulations

While Regulation O is the most comprehensive set of rules governing insider transactions, the following provides an overview of other laws and regulations pertaining to insiders that were not discussed within the main section of the handbook. Examiners and bankers should not rely on these summaries as a substitute for referring to the full text of laws and regulations.

12 USC 376 – Rate of Interest Paid to Insiders

This law prohibits a bank from paying to any director, officer, attorney, or employee a greater rate of interest on deposits than that paid to other depositors with similar deposits.

12 USC 1817(k) – Reports and Disclosure by Banks of Extensions of Credit to Executive Officers or Principal Shareholders or Their Related Interests

This law authorizes the appropriate federal banking agencies to issue rules and regulations requiring the reporting and public disclosure by banks of extensions of credit to insiders.

12 USC 1818 – Enforcement Authority Against Institution-Affiliated Parties

This law authorizes the OCC to take various enforcement actions against a broad range of insiders (defined in 12 USC 1813(u)) for violations of law, regulation, cease and desist orders, conditions imposed in writing by the OCC, or written agreements with the OCC; engaging in unsafe or unsound practices; or breaches of fiduciary duty

12 USC 1831i and 12 CFR 5.51 – Proposed Changes in Directors and Senior Executive Officers

This law requires depository institutions that are not in compliance with minimum capital requirements or are designated as being in "troubled condition" to file a notice of changes in directors or senior executive officers.

12 USC 1972 – Certain Tying Arrangements Prohibited; Correspondent Accounts

This law prohibits a bank and its correspondent bank from making preferential loans and loans that involve more than the normal risk of repayment or present other unfavorable terms to an insider of the other bank. It also prohibits a bank from opening a correspondent account at another bank where either bank has outstanding a preferential loan, or a loan that involves more than the normal risk of repayment or presents other unfavorable features, to an insider of the other.

12 USC 3202 through 3203 and 12 CFR 26 – Management Interlocks

With a goal of fostering competition, this law generally prohibits depository institutions that compete in the same geographic market from sharing officers and directors if the institutions are not affiliated with each other. In addition, a management official of a bank with total assets exceeding $2.5 billion may not serve at the same time as a management official of an unaffiliated depository organization with total assets exceeding $1.5 billion, regardless of the locations of the two depository organizations. The OCC has the authority to exempt an otherwise prohibited interlock if it finds that the interlock will not produce a monopoly or a substantial lessening of competition.

12 CFR 2 – Disposition of Credit Life Insurance Income

This regulation prohibits employees, officers, directors, and principal shareholders from retaining commissions and other income from the sale of credit life, accident, and health insurance to loan customers and provides that it is unsafe and unsound for such insiders to personally profit from such sales. In addition, it sets forth guidance for bonus and incentive plans based on the sale of credit life insurance.

12 CFR 31 – Extensions of Credit to National Bank Insiders

This regulation is OCC's implementing regulation for 12 USC 375a and 375b. It generally requires national banks to comply with 12 CFR 215, Regulation O. It also states that the OCC administers and enforces insider rules for national banks.

Appendix D

Acceptance of Items of Value

It may be appropriate for a bank insider to accept something of value from someone doing or seeking to do business with the bank. The bank's written policies may authorize an insider to accept an item if it:

- Is offered based on a family or personal relationship, independent of any bank business;
- Is available to the general public on the same conditions; or
- Would be paid for by the bank as a reasonable business expense if not paid for by another party.

Under these circumstances, there is generally no risk to the bank. Common examples of these types of items include a business luncheon or holiday season gift. The bank's written policies may also permit acceptance of:

- **Meals, gratuities, amenities, or favors based on obvious family or personal relationships.** The circumstances should make it clear that the relationship, rather than the business of the bank, is the motivating factor.

- **Meals, refreshments, travel arrangements, accommodations, or entertainment of reasonable value in the course of a meeting or other occasion.** In this case, the occasion must be for a bona fide business discussion or part of an effort to foster better business relations, and the expense should be one the bank would pay as a reasonable business expense if not being paid by another party. The bank may wish to establish a dollar limit on arrangements accepted under this exception.

- **Advertising or promotional material of reasonable value, including pens, pencils, note pads, key chains, calendars, and similar items.**

- **Discounts or rebates on merchandise or services that are available to other customers under similar circumstances.**

- **Gifts of reasonable value related to commonly recognized events or occasions such as a promotion, new job, wedding, retirement,**

Christmas, or bar or bat mitzvah. The bank may wish to establish a dollar limit on the value of such gifts.

- **Civic, charitable, educational, or religious organizational awards for recognition of service and accomplishment.** The bank may wish to establish a dollar limit on such awards.

- **Loans from other banks or financial institutions, when made on customary terms for the purpose of financing proper and usual activities of bank insiders.** Insiders must ensure that financial arrangements are not contingent upon either bank accepting or offering any other service. Some insiders must also ensure that they do not receive preferential loans from correspondent banks and must report to their board of directors loans received from other financial institutions as required by 12 CFR 215.9 and 215.22.

- **Other benefits or items of value, when approved in writing, case by case.** Approvals should be based on a full, written disclosure of all relevant facts and should be consistent with the bank bribery statute (18 USC 215).

The OCC has not set a dollar limit on the value of items that may be accepted by insiders. Reasonable standards for one part of the country might appear lavish elsewhere. Each national bank should establish dollar limits on the benefits insiders are allowed to accept. In setting those limits, the bank should observe the highest ethical standards.

A bank's insider policies should require an insider who is offered, or who receives, something of greater value than is authorized, to disclose that fact to an appropriately designated official of the bank. The bank should maintain written reports of such disclosures, in whatever format the bank deems appropriate.

Appendix E — Report of Indebtedness (FFIEC Form 004)

This form appears for informational purposes only. To access the PDF version, please go to http://www.ffiec.gov/forms004.htm.

Board of Governors of the Federal Reserve System
Office of the Comptroller of the Currency
Federal Deposit Insurance Corporation
Office of Thrift Supervision

Report on Indebtedness of Executive Officers and Principal Shareholders and their Related Interests to Correspondent Banks (Form FFIEC 004)

A. For the Calendar Year Ending December 31, _____
To be submitted to your bank's board of directors by January 31.

Report the Maximum Amount of Indebtedness Outstanding at Any Time During the Reporting Year, Even if Fully Repaid. Please Read Carefully the Instructions on the Reverse Side of this Report.

Form FFIEC 004

OMB No. 7100—0034 (FRB)   Expires 3/31/2004
1557—0070 (OCC)   Expires 3/31/2004
3064—0023 (FDIC)   Expires 3/31/2004
1550—0075 (OTS)   Expires 3/31/2004

To be submitted by executive officers and principal shareholders of insured banks in satisfaction of the reporting requirements of the Federal Reserve Board's Regulation O (12 CFR Part 215) and as incorporated by the Office of Thrift Supervision (12 CFR Part 563.43), and Part 349 of the Federal Deposit Insurance Corporation's Rules and Regulations (12 CFR Part 349) with respect to indebtedness to correspondent banks and savings associations. The FFIEC 004 report is not submitted to the agencies but is collected and retained by the bank. In this regard, the agencies' examiners may review and obtain copies of such reports during an examination. The reports in the possession of the agencies may be exempt from disclosure under sections (b)(4), (6), and (8) of the Freedom of Information Act (5 U.S.C. 552 (b)(4), (6), and (8)).

B. Name of Executive Officer _____ or Principal Shareholder _____ Submitting Report (Please check one)

C. If the Report is Submitted for Indebtedness of a Related Interest, Name and Address of Related Interest for Which the Report is Submitted

D. Name of Bank to which Report is Submitted

City _____   State _____

E. Name and Address of Correspondent Bank	F. Original Amount	G. Range of Interest Rates (%)	H. Repayment Terms	I. Maturity Date	J. Description of Collateral (If unsecured indicate "none")	K. Balance (10 days prior to this report) (in thousands of dollars)	L. Maximum Amount of Indebtedness Outstanding in Previous Calendar Year (indicate method used) (in thousands of dollars)	M. Other Terms (if unusual)

N. I hereby certify that the information given above is complete, correct, and true to the best of my knowledge.

Signature of official responsible for report _____

Date Signed _____

Disclosure of Estimated Burden

The burden associated with this information collection is estimated to vary from 1 to 2 hours per response, depending on individual circumstances. Burden estimates include the time for reviewing instructions, gathering and maintaining data in the required form, and completing the information collection, but exclude the time for compiling and maintaining business records in the normal course of a respondent's activities. A Federal agency may not conduct or sponsor, and an organization (or a person) is not required to respond to a collection of information, unless it displays a currently valid OMB control number. Comments concerning the accuracy of this burden estimate and suggestions for reducing this burden should be directed to the Office of Information and Regulatory Affairs, Office of Management and Budget, Washington, D.C. 20503, and to one of the following:

Secretary
Board of Governors of the Federal Reserve System
Washington, D.C. 20551

Legislative and Regulatory Analysis Division
Office of the Comptroller of the Currency
Washington, D.C. 20219

Assistant Executive Secretary
Federal Deposit Insurance Corporation
Washington, D.C. 20429

Supervision Policy
Office of Thrift Supervision
Washington, D.C. 20552

Instructions

Why Report

The Financial Institutions Regulatory and Interest Rate Control Act of 1978, as amended by the Garn-St. Germain Depository Institutions Act of 1982, prohibits preferential lending by a bank to certain insiders of another bank when there is a correspondent account relationship between the banks. Regulation 0, 12 CFR Part 215, which implements these statutes, specifies the reporting requirements necessary to ensure compliance.

Terms used in this report are defined in Regulation 0 and 12 CFR Part 349. The Office of Thrift Supervision has incorporated Regulation 0 by reference at 12 CFR 563.43 and applies Regulation 0, with the exception of 12 CFR 215.13, to savings associations in the same manner and to the same extent as if the association were a bank or member bank. As used in this report, the term bank should be read to include savings associations.

Noncompliance with the reporting requirements of Regulation 0 could result in civil money penalties for the bank and the reporting executive officer or principal shareholder.

Who Must Report

Executive officers and principal shareholders must report extensions of credit outstanding during the calendar year from correspondent banks of their insured bank. Executive officers and principal shareholders must also report extensions of credit from correspondent banks to their related interests.

How to Report

The reports may be filed on Form 004, Report on Indebtedness to Correspondent Banks, or any form containing identical information. The information must be submitted to the board of directors with a copy maintained at the bank.

When to Report

Reports must be submitted annually by January 31 for the calendar year ending December 31 of the previous year.

What to Report

Executive officers and principal shareholders must report all indebtedness to correspondent banks, including indebtedness of their related interests. Loans that were outstanding at any time during the reporting calendar year must be reported, even if they have been paid off.

Completing the Form

A. **Report Date.** Enter the calendar year for which you are reporting.

Name of Executive Officer or Principal Shareholder. Enter your name. (A person who is not an executive officer or principal shareholder at the time the report is required to be filed is not required to file.)

An "executive officer" is defined in section 215.2(e) of Regulation 0 and generally means an individual who participates or has authority to participate (other than in the capacity of a director) in major policymaking functions of the company or bank, whether or not the officer has an official title, the title designates the officer as an assistant, or the officer is serving without salary or compensation. Certain categories of bank officers (e.g., vice president) are presumed in Regulation 0 to be executive officers unless the officer is excluded by resolution of the board of directors or by the bylaws of the bank or company from participation in major policymaking functions of the bank or company, and the officer does not actually participate therein.

A *"principal shareholder of a member bank"* as defined in section 215.11)a)(1) means any person (other than an insured bank, or a foreign bank as defined in 12 USC 3101(7)) that, directly or indirectly, owns, controls, or has power to vote more than 10 percent of any class of voting securities of the member bank. The term includes a person that controls a principal shareholder (e.g., a person that controls a bank holding company). Shares of a bank (including a foreign bank), bank holding company, or other company owned or controlled by a member of an individual's immediate family are presumed to be owned or controlled by the individual for the purposes of determining principal shareholder status.

"Immediate family" as defined in section 215.2(g) means the spouse of an individual, the individual's minor children, and any of the individual's children (including adult children) residing in the individual's home. For reporting purposes, only one individual in the immediate family must file a report if that individual's report includes the required information on indebtedness of his/her immediate family.

Related Interests. If you are reporting indebtedness of a related interest, enter the name and address of the related interest. You must complete a separate report for each related interest.

A *"related interest"* as defined in section 215.11(a))2) means (1) any company controlled by a natural person, or (2) any political or campaign committee controlled by a natural person or the funds or services of which will benefit a natural person.

"Control" of a company is defined generally in section 215.2(c) of Regulation 0 as ownership or control of 25 percent or more of a company's outstanding voting shares. Control is presumed, however, in certain cases where less than 25 percent ownership exists.

The term *"indebtedness"* includes any extension of credit (as defined in section 215.3 of Regulation 0), but does not include: (1) commercial paper, bonds and debentures issued in the ordinary course of business; and (2) consumer credit in an aggregate amount of $5,000 or less from each

---

correspondent bank, provided the credit is incurred under terms that are not more favorable than those offered the general public.

D. **Reporting Bank.** Enter the name of the bank in which you are an executive officer or principal shareholder.

E. **Correspondent Bank.** Enter the correspondent bank's name and address. You may report indebtedness from more than one correspondent bank on the same form. You also may include the loan number or any other relevant identifying information in this column.

A "correspondent bank" generally means a bank that maintains one or more correspondent accounts for the officer's or principal shareholder's bank that in the aggregate exceed an average daily balance during the reporting calendar year of $100,000 or 0.5 percent of the officer's or principal shareholder's bank's total deposits (as reported in the bank's first Consolidated Report of Condition or Thrift Financial Report during the calendar year), whichever is smaller. *All insured banks are required by law to make available to their executive officers and principal shareholders a list of their correspondent banks.*

F. **Original Amount.** Enter the original amount of the loan. If the indebtedness is a line of credit, report the maximum authorized amount.

G. **Range of Interest Rates.** Enter the range of interest rates charged throughout the reporting year.

H. **Repayment Terms.** Describe the repayment terms.

I. **Maturity Date.** Enter the maturity date.

J. **Description of Collateral.** If the loan is secured, describe the collateral and its value.

K. **Balance.** Enter the amount of indebtedness outstanding to the correspondent bank as of ten business days before the date of the report. If this balance is not available, or cannot be readily ascertained by the filing date, estimate the amount and provide the actual amount to the board of directors within thirty days.

L. **Maximum Amount of Indebtedness.** The maximum amount of indebtedness is either (1) the highest outstanding indebtedness during the calendar year for which the report is made, or (2) the highest end of the month indebtedness outstanding during the calendar year for which the report is made. You must consistently use the same method for all indebtedness to the same correspondent bank. You also must indicate whether the maximum amount was determined as of the end of the month or on a daily basis.

M. **Other Terms.** Describe any unusual terms or other conditions of the loan.

N. **Signature.** Sign and date the report.

References

Auditing Requirements
    Regulations   12 CFR 363
    OCC Issuances   OCC 2003-12
                                     OCC 99-37
                                     "Internal and External Audits,"
                                     Comptroller's Handbook,
                                     April 2003
                                     "Large Bank Supervision,"
                                     Comptroller's Handbook,
                                     May 2001
                                     "Community Bank Supervision,"
                                     Comptroller's Handbook,
                                     July 2003

Bank Fraud
    Laws   18 USC 1344

Compensation of Insiders
    Regulations   12 CFR 30
    OCC Issuances   OCC 2004-56

Correspondent Banks
    Laws   12 USC 1972(2)
    Regulations   12 CFR 31
                                     12 CFR 215

Credit Life Insurance
    Regulations   12 CFR 2

Depository Institution Management Interlocks
    Laws   12 USC 3201
    Regulations   12 CFR 26

External Audits
    Regulations   12 CFR 363
    OCC Issuances   OCC 2003-12
                                     OCC 99-37
                                     "Internal and External Audits,"

Comptroller's Handbook,
April 2003
"Large Bank Supervision,"
Comptroller's Handbook,
May 2001
"Community Bank Supervision,"
Comptroller's Handbook,
July 2003

False Statements
    Laws   18 USC 1014

Indemnification of Directors, Officers, and Employees
    Regulations   12 CFR 7.2014

Institution-Affiliated Parties
    Laws   12 USC 1813(u), 1818(e)

Interest Paid to Directors, etc.
    Laws   12 USC 376

Liability of Directors and Officers of Member Banks
    Laws   12 USC 503

Loans of Trust Funds to Officers and Employees
    Laws   12 USC 92a(h)

Loans to Executive Officers
    Laws   12 USC 375a
    Regulations   12 CFR 31
                                           12 CFR 215

Loans to Executive Officers, Directors, and Principal Shareholders
    Laws   12 USC 375b
    Regulations   12 CFR 31
                                           12 CFR 215
    OCC Issuances   Interpretive Letter 1024

Management Information Systems
    OCC Issuances   *FFIEC Information Technology*
                                           Examination Handbook

Purchases from or Sales to Directors
    Laws   12 USC 375

Reports and Public Disclosure by Banks of Extensions of Credit to Insiders
    Laws   12 USC 1817(k)
    Regulations   12 CFR 215

Receipt of Commissions or Gifts for Procuring Loans
    Laws   18 USC 215

Related Interests
    Laws   12 USC 375b
    Regulations   12 CFR 31, 12 CFR 215
    OCC Issuances   "Related Organizations," *Comptroller's Handbook,* August 2004

Role of A National Bank Director
    OCC Issuances   *The Director's Book,* March 1997

Safety and Soundness Standards
    Regulations   12 CFR 30

Self-Dealing (Fiduciary Accounts)
    Regulations   12 CFR 9.12

Suspicious Activity Reporting
    Regulation   12 CFR 21.11

Theft, Embezzlement or Misapplication by Bank Officer or Employee
    Laws   18 USC 656

Uniform Interagency Rating System
    OCC Issuances   OCC 97 - 1